Math Song and More for Kids

Words, Music and Illustrated by

Dite Lin

Table of Contents

Preface

The songs in this book were written in April and May of 2020, during the Shelter in Place period due to Coronavirus, while all students learned from home. I am a first grade student at the Guadalupe Elementary School in San Jose, California. I miss my friends and teachers at school and the music school. I wrote these songs because the contents brought me memories of school learning and playing activities. I love art as well so I included a drawing for each song. I hope this book can inspire kids to enjoy math, science, art, crafts, music and sports, all kinds of learning subjects.

I would like to thank the teachers at the Music School (themusicschool.org) for teaching me music theory and making learning music an exciting experience.

Dite Lin

Sunnyvale, June 2020

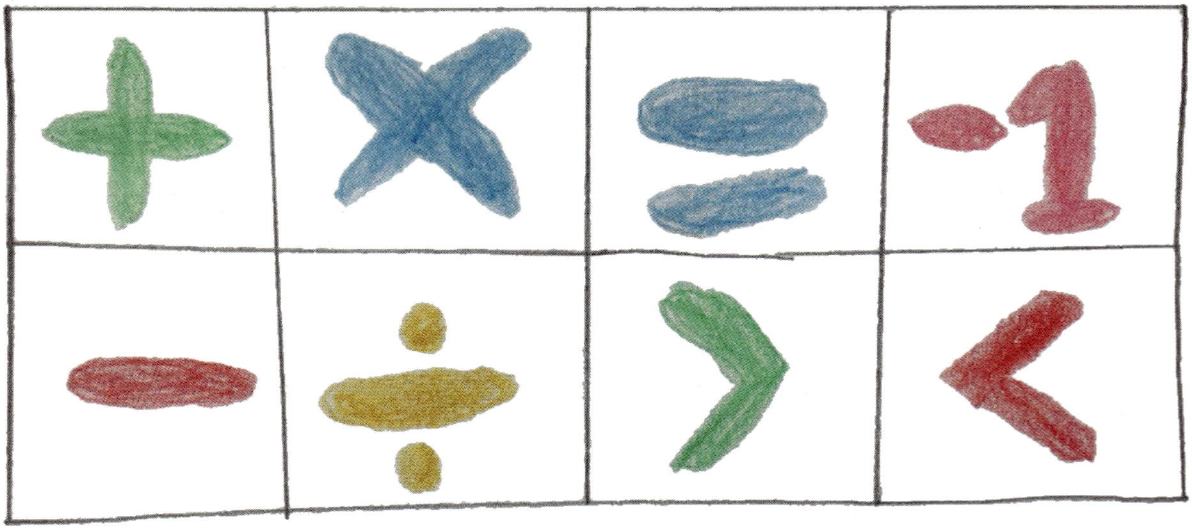
+
×
=
-1
−
÷
>
<

Math Song

Ad- ding num- bers high and low,

sub- trac- ting num- bers, make them go!

Mul- ti- ply- ing num- bers is a plus game,

Di- vi- ding num- bers make a few the same.

E- qual sign in eve- ry math ques- tion,

and so is grea- ter than.

Ne- ga- tive num- bers un- der ze- ro,

but was- n't less than.

Science Song

Phy- sics stu- dies laws of na- ture,

and Hy- drau- lics, po- wer of wa- ter.

Bi- o- lo- gy, the know- ledge of lives,

As- tro- no- my stu- dies star and pla- net lives.

Ge- o- lo- gy stu- dies the Earth.

Che- mis- try stu- dies mat- ter.

Vi- ro- lo- gy stu- dies vi- rus.

Phy- sics an- swers why there's an- ti- mat- ter.

Art Song

You can draw pic- tures of a tree,

a bus, a horse, some grapes and a bee.

You can draw pic- tures in a book,

and you can draw them of a hook.

You can draw or paint them most,

fin- ger paint, as told by the host.

Paint your pic- ture that you like best.

If you are tired, then take a rest.

Painting Song

Pain- tings al- ways are not bor- ing.

Wait for the bell to ring.

Paint a pic- ture or fin- ger paint,

some- thing cra- zy that will make you faint.

Paint your art, try your best.

If you're tired, take a rest.

Paint a pic- ture of what you like,

for ex- am- ple, your own bike.

Music Song

Start with how ma- ny beats,

and make sure it is neat.

Then a quar- ter note, a half note dot,

make a mea- sure we sing a lot.

A two- eighth, and a half note,

one quar- ter, is what I vote.

I can find the rhyme

if I have en- ough time.

Earth Day Song

The pla- net Earth is a beau- ti- ful place,

and it is eve- ry- one's home space.

We need to pro- tect our sweet home,

by do- ing good things un- der sky dome.

I walk, I run, I ride a bike,

plan- ting trees is what I like.

And I re- duce, re- use, and re- cy- cle,

all things to im- prove Earth cy- cle.

Craft Song

You can make crafts of a fox,

a lamp, a board, a can and a box.

When you make crafts, if you need help,

you may re- use but don't ev- er yelp.

You can make cool science crafts,

be- fore ma- king them need some drafts.

You can make crafts a- bout Earth Day.

You can make a- ny- thing that you like. Yay!

Push-up Song

If you want ex- er- cise hard,

you can use the push- up bar.

Eve- ry- bo- dy can do this,

You can count them, don't give a kiss.

You can go on af- ter a break,

un- til you get a tum- my ache.

You can do one hun- dred or,

you can go, please, that's what it's for.

Sit-up Song

You can start when- e- ver you like,

you can count them, don't ride a bike.

You lay down, on your back,

then You sit up, for a snack.

This is part of ex- er- ci- sing,

it is not part of plant- ing.

You can do a hun- dred,

un- til you feel ex- haust- ed.

Running Laps Song

Run a lap, run a lap,

run a lap and do not nap!

Run- ning laps is a part

of ex- er- cise but not art.

For- ward, turn, for- ward, turn,

for- ward, turn, but not get burn.

For- ward, turn, more and more,

run more laps and arms aren't sore.

Dance Song

Dance, dance, dance, pose, pose, pose.

By the mu- sic, you can dance.

You can dance, you can pose.

Go a- head, you have a chance.

Dance and pose, dance and pose.

There's a song here, not a rose.

You could dance, and sing a song.

You could pose, and sing a- long.

Singapore Math

vol.7

Singapore Song

Sin- ga- pore song, Sin- ga- pore song,

Sin- ga- pore song, a sing a- long.

The Sin- ga- pore song, Sin- ga- pore math,

Sin- ga- pore frac- tions, my lear- ning path.

Sin- ga- pore math, from Sin- ga- pore,

Sin- ga- pore math, learn more and more.

Sin- ga- pore frac- tions, Sin- ga- pore frac- tions,

lot of math to learn with ac- tions.

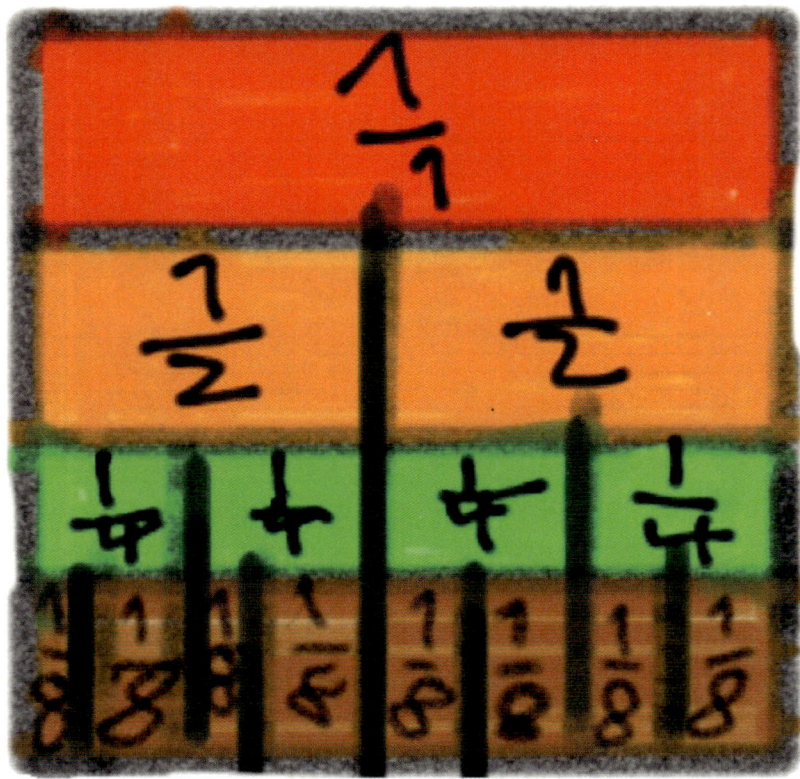

Fraction Song

A whole is a frac- tion we will start.

A half is split in- to two parts.

One di- vid- ed by three, one o- ver three.

Let's climb up the frac- tion tree.

A quar- ter is one forth, a fan shaped chart.

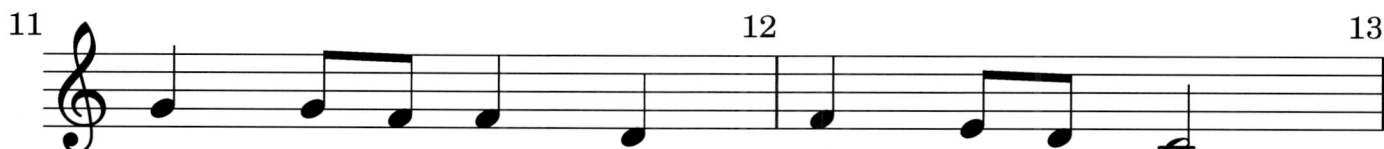

One sixth is one of six e- qual parts.

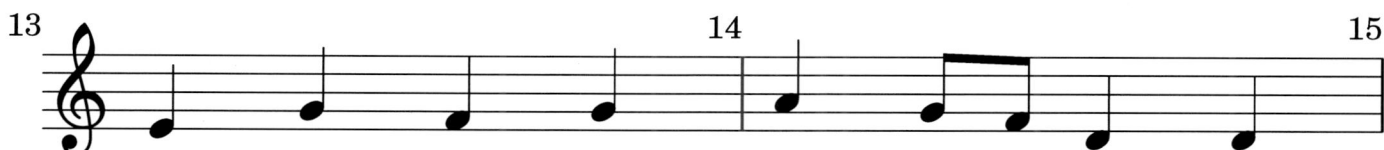

One eighth is a half of a quar- ter,

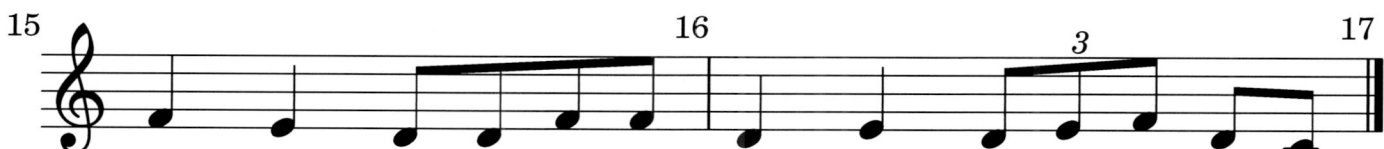

One, the nu- me- ra- tor, eight, the de- no- mi- na- tor.

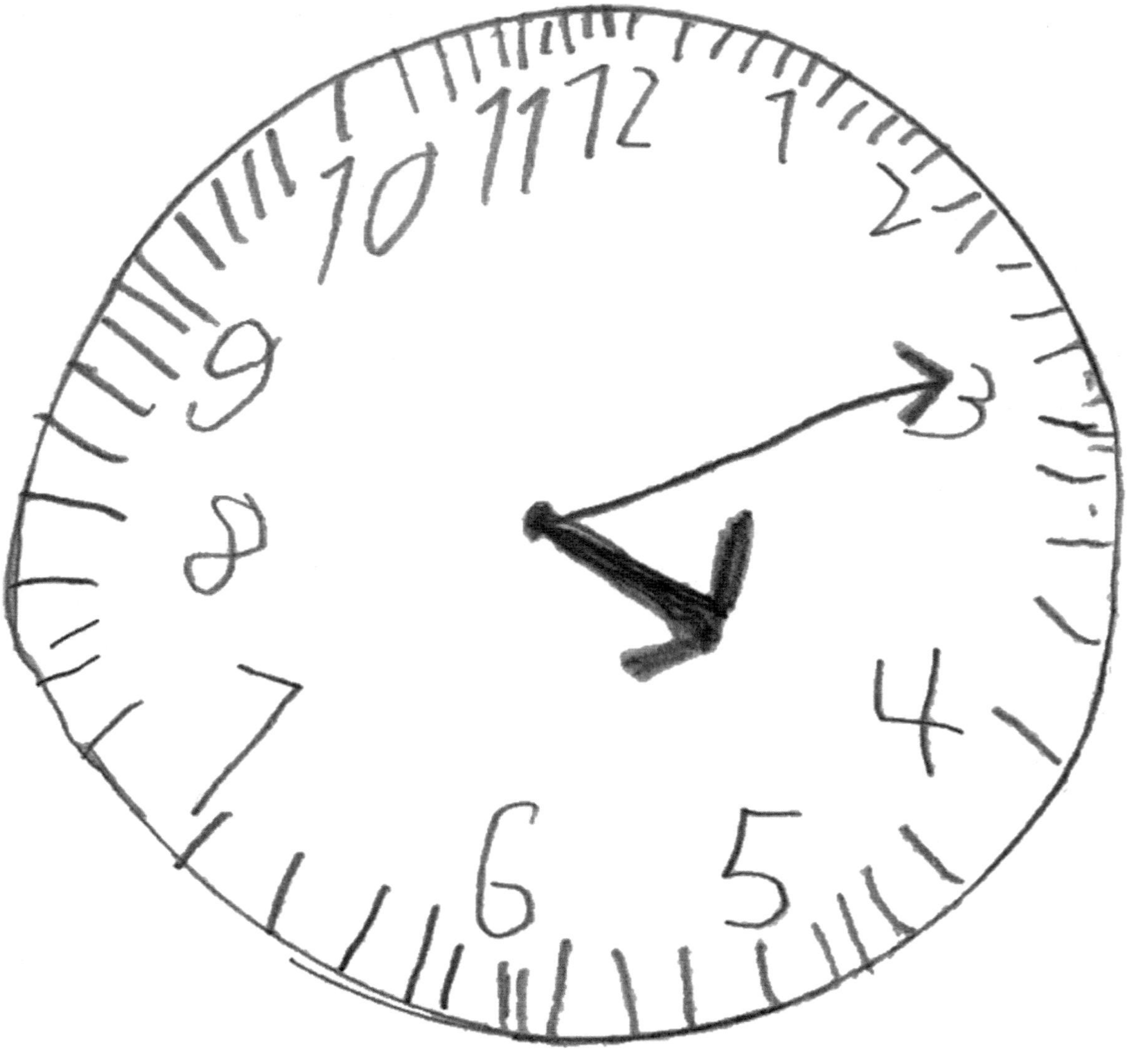
10 11 12 1 2 3 4 5 6 7 8 9

Clock Song

We wake up at eight thir- ty A M.

We eat break- fast at nine A M.

We stu- dy at nine thir- ty A M.

We take a break at ten thir- ty A M.

We eat lunch at e- le- ven A M.

We stu- dy more at e- le- ven thir- ty A M.

We ex- er- cise at three P M.

We eat din- ner at five P M.

Liberty Song

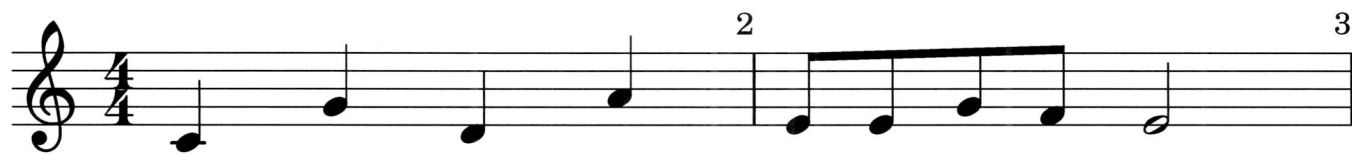

Bald ea- gles are car- ni- vo- rus birds.

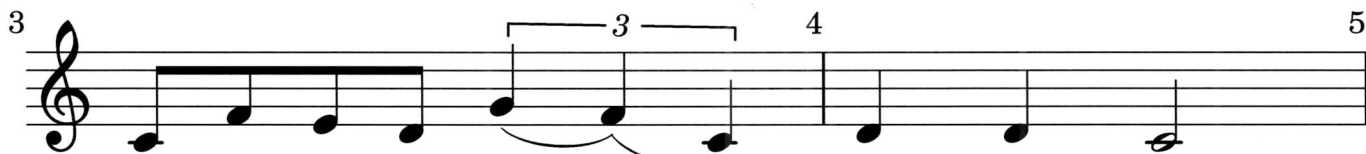

The Sta- tue of Liberty has some words.

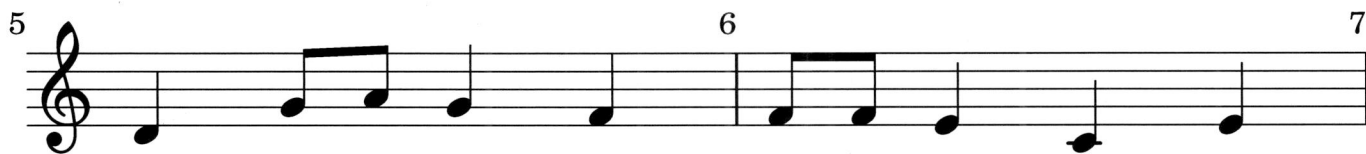

The li- ber- ty bell has a lit- tle crack.

The A- me- ri- ca flag flaps forth and back.

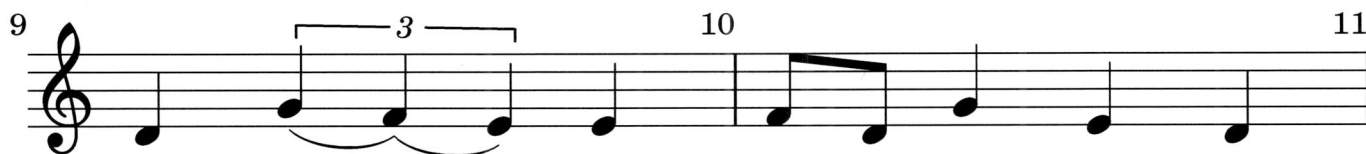

The washington and Lin- coln mo- nu- ments

are his- to- ric en- ligh- ten- ments.

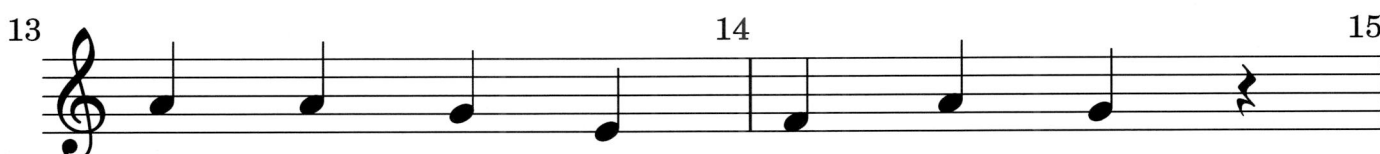

The White House is co- lored white,

as the pre- si- dent's home is al- ways bright.

Endless Song

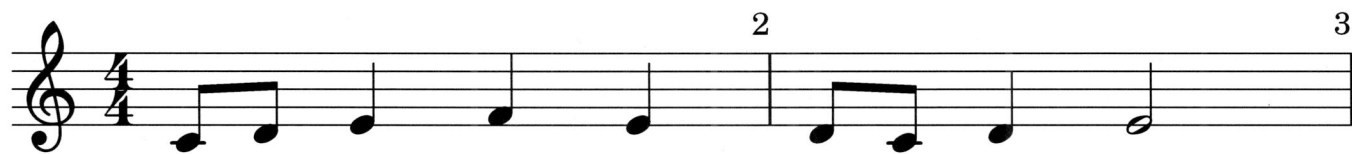

If you farm a crop, you can farm corn.

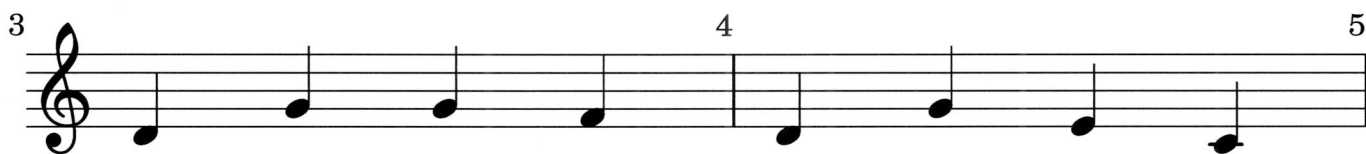

You farm the corn, look like a horn.

If you farm a crop, you can farm wheat.

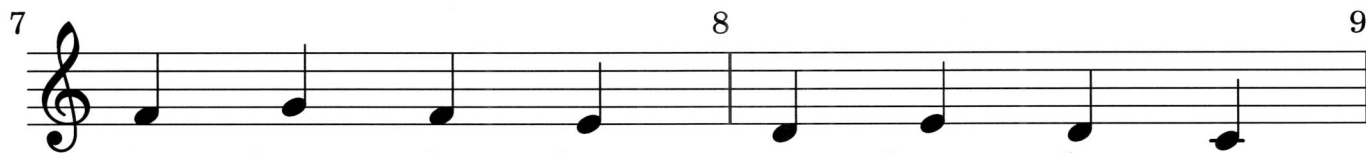

You farm the wheat, you hear the tweet.

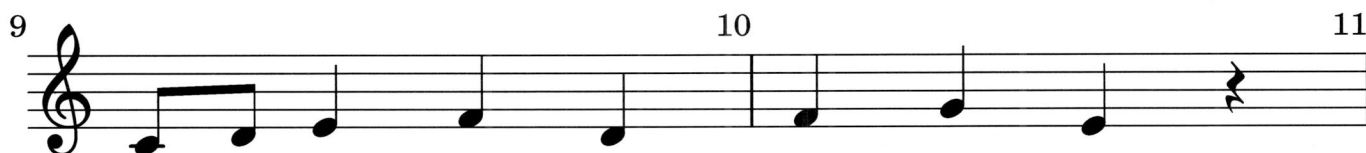

You're at the play-ground, you're not out,

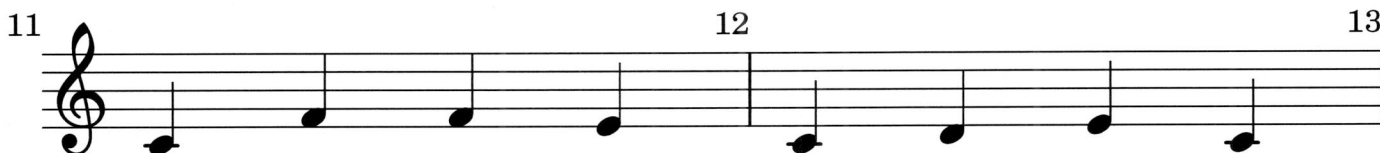

the slide and stairs are all a-bout.

There are ev-en lad-ders and swings.

There is some-one with some rings.

If you're at the park, you can play,

you can play and play all day.

Oh, there's some fun.

You can play un- der the sun.

You can read books at the lib- ra- ry.

You can read more, with snack cher- ry.

You can look in a book.

You can look, you can look.

If you would plant, it could be a tree,

but don't get your-self stune by a bee.

It can have fruits or a nest,

it could al-ways be the best.

Oh, your sweet, sweet home,

is far a-way from where you roam.

Oh, it's your place to live,

a place where you can give.

Made in the USA
Las Vegas, NV
08 February 2021